# MATH
## Curriculum
## *for Gifted Students*

GRADE
**3**

Lessons, Activities, and Extensions for Gifted and Advanced Learners

# Student Workbook
# Sections I-II

CENTER FOR GIFTED EDUCATION
WITH MARGARET JESS MCKOWEN PATTI

William & Mary
School of Education

CENTER FOR GIFTED EDUCATION
P.O. Box 8795
Williamsburg, VA 23187

First published in 2020 by Prufrock Press Inc.

Published in 2021 by Routledge
605 Third Avenue, New York, NY 10017
2 Park Square, Milton Park, Abingdon, Oxon OX14 4RN

*Routledge is an imprint of the Taylor & Francis Group, an informa business.*

ISBN: 9781646320219

Routledge
Taylor & Francis Group

NEW YORK AND LONDON

# TABLE OF CONTENTS

# LESSON 1.1 ACTIVITY
## Budget Plans for Businesses

**Directions:** Complete the steps below.

Today, you will work with a partner to decide on a business idea and business name for an outdoor community market day. It is now time to begin your business plans. Remember, a business always wants to pay off any debt first, and then make a profit. Wise decisions are a must! Who is up for the challenge? Fill in your business name and type on the lines below.

Name of Business: _____

Type of Business: _____

Businesses will be loaned $350 for start-up costs. Take a look at the table below, which displays the necessities your business can purchase, and decide on the three most important necessities to buy.

| Necessities | Cost |
|---|---|
| Table for displaying items | $119 |
| Sign for advertising | $43 |
| Items to sell | $87 |
| Employee to work the table | $122 |
| Cash register | $24 |
| Tent to provide shade | $58 |

Write the three start-up necessities in the space below.

1. _____

_____

2. _____

_____

3. _____

_____

Once you have decided which three necessities will be purchased, discuss the following questions with your partner and write a response to each.

1. You were told to choose three necessities to purchase.
   a. How much money did your business spend on the three necessities? _____
   b. How many hundreds? _____
   c. How many tens? _____
   d. How many ones? _____

2. How much money do you have left for additional purchases?
   a. How many hundreds? _____
   b. How many tens? _____
   c. How many ones? _____

3. About how much money would you need to purchase all of the necessities listed in the table? _____ Explain how you developed your estimate.

4. Suppose you and your partner decided to purchase a sign and table for your new business. A few days later, you realize it is supposed to rain on the day of the outdoor market, so you use some of your remaining start-up money to purchase a tent.
   a. How much money did you and your partner spend? _____ Write a number sentence to show your purchases.

   b. Now, suppose a competing business purchased a tent and a sign, but a few days later, its owners decide they also needed a table to display their product. How much money did the competing business spend? _____ Write a number sentence to show its purchases.

   c. Explain how the sums in Parts A and B are equal using the associative property.

5. You and your partner disagree on how to estimate for the total cost of all of necessities on the list.

   a. When estimating the total of all necessities, your partner says that the price of the table, which is $119, should be rounded to $100. You disagree and say that the price of the table should be rounded to $120. What can you infer about each business partner's approach to the estimation?

   b. Model your partner's approach to the problem by using the number line provided to round.

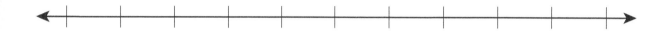

   c. Model your approach to the problem by using the provided number line provided to round.

**Extend Your Thinking**

1. If you were loaned $420, what additional necessities could you have purchased for your business along with the three you originally chose?

2. Now that you have started your business, it is time to determine what you will sell at the outdoor market in your local community. Think about items that people would likely purchase while walking around a market. List three items that you plan to sell and decide how much you will charge for each item. How should you use the start-up cost in the calculation? Explain why you chose each price for your three items and how your decision is related to the start-up cost.

# LESSON 1.1 PRACTICE
## Place Value and Rounding

**Directions:** Complete the problems below.

1. Demetria is bringing candy as a surprise to all 396 kids in her school. Demetria would like for each student to receive one piece of candy. The candy is sold in bags of 50 pieces per bag. How should she determine the number of bags of candy to buy? Justify your answer by providing proof.

2. Compose a word problem in which estimation would be the best method to solve.

3. Compose a word problem in which a precise answer would be the best method to solve.

4. What is 12.6 rounded to the nearest whole number? _____

5. Using the digits 6, 7, 8, and 9, complete each number sentence. A digit can only be used once in each number sentence.

   a. ____ ____ + ____ ____ = 147

   b. ____ ____ + ____ ____ = 174

   c. ____ ____ + ____ ____ = 165

6. Is there any other way to arrange the digits in Question 5C and still get a sum of 165? Explain your answer.

7. Read the clues below.

| I composed three hundreds out of 30 tens and had 2 tens left over. |
| --- |
| I didn't need to compose any additional tens because all I had were 5 ones. |

   a. What number is being described? _____
   b. Round the number being described to the nearest ten and then subtract it from 500. What is the difference? _____

8. Read the clues below.

| 2 thousands | 21 hundreds | 9 tens | 4 ones |
| --- | --- | --- | --- |

   a. What number is being described? _____
   b. Round the number being described to the nearest hundred and then subtract it from 5,000. What is the difference? _____

9. Read the clues below.

| 1 hundreds | 28 tens | 5 ones |
| --- | --- | --- |

   a. What number is being described? _____

10. Rebekah has saved 2,654 pennies. Claudia has saved 169 pennies.
   a. About how many pennies has Rebekah saved? _____
   b. About how many pennies has Claudia saved? _____
   c. Precisely how many more pennies do Rebekah and Claudia need in order to reach a total of 3,000 pennies? _____

## Extend Your Thinking

1. Problem 5 required you to determine the missing numbers. How does looking at the sum help you strategically place the digits?

2. Create a place value question. Give a peer any four digits to arrange to get a specific sum. Use the above problems as a guide to creating your question, and be sure to include an answer key.

# LESSON 1.1
# Assessment Practice

1. On Monday, José spent 27 minutes on math homework, and he read for 43 minutes. He spent the exact same time on math and reading during Tuesday night's homework as he did on Monday night.
   a. Round the time to get an estimate on the number of minutes José spent on homework for Monday night and Tuesday night all together.


   b. About how many hours did José spend? _____

2. Kendrick said that he had 177 more tickets for the school fair than his friend Tommy, who only had 81 tickets.
   a. How many tickets did Kendrick have for the school fair? _____
   b. About how many tickets did Kendrick and Tommy have all together? Round the numbers to get an estimated answer. _____


   c. The oversized stuffed giraffe at the fair requires 159 more tickets than Kendrick currently has saved. How many tickets does it take to purchase the giraffe? _____


   d. If Tommy gives Kendrick all of his tickets, how many more tickets would Kendrick still have to save to purchase the giraffe? _____


3. On Saturday, two basketball teams played against each other. The winning team scored 40 points during the game, and the losing team scored 23 points.
   a. How many more points did the winning team score than the losing team? _____


   b. Estimate how many total points were scored during the basketball game. _____

# LESSON 1.2 ACTIVITY
# Mind Readers

**Directions:** It is time to use your mathematical mind to determine what your partner is thinking! Work with a partner to play Mind Readers. Decide who will be Player A and who will be Player B.

1. Player A: Think of a secret multiplication problem that follows these rules: One factor must be a two-digit multiple of 10 and the other factor must be a one-digit number. For example, 60 × 4 = 240.

2. Player A: Solve your secret multiplication problem using place value knowledge. Record your secret multiplication problem on your Mind Readers Chart. Next, describe the product using place value terms to your partner. Record your description on the chart. For example, to describe 240, you could say, "Twenty-four tens."

3. Student B: Write the number that is being described using place value terms in standard form. Record the standard form of the number on your Mind Readers chart. Use the description of the product to determine the possible secret multiplication problems. Student B should remember:
   ▪ One factor had to be a two-digit multiple of 10.
   ▪ One factor had to be a one-digit number.

4. Student B: You are also determining all of the different factors your partner could have thought of based on the described product. If you and your partner disagree with the multiplication problems, you must discuss if an error was made, or if there was more than one possible answer.

5. Once Student B gets the correct multiplication problem, switch roles.

After playing the game, discuss the following and respond.

1. Think about the practice problems you completed while playing the game. What patterns do you recognize?

2. Discuss and explain why you believe some numbers had more than one correct multiplication sentence that could result with the same product.

**Extend Your Thinking**

1. Play Mind Readers using new rules. One factor must be a three-digit multiple of 10, and the other factor must be a two- or three-digit number.

2. Explain how you are able to solve the problems by drawing Base Ten blocks to demonstrate the place value relationship.

# LESSON 1.2
## Mind Readers Chart

### PLAYER A

**Round 1 Player A**

| Secret Multiplication Problem | Standard Form | Describe Product in Place Value Terms | Possible Factors That Could Result in the Product |
|---|---|---|---|
| | | | |

**Round 2 Player A**

| Secret Multiplication Problem | Standard Form | Describe Product in Place Value Terms | Possible Factors That Could Result in the Product |
|---|---|---|---|
| | | | |

**Round 3 Player A**

| Secret Multiplication Problem | Standard Form | Describe Product in Place Value Terms | Possible Factors That Could Result in the Product |
|---|---|---|---|
| | | | |

# LESSON 1.2
## Mind Readers Chart

### PLAYER B

**Round 1 Player B**

| Secret Multiplication Problem | Standard Form | Describe Product in Place Value Terms | Possible Factors That Could Result in the Product |
|---|---|---|---|
| | | | |

**Round 2 Player B**

| Secret Multiplication Problem | Standard Form | Describe Product in Place Value Terms | Possible Factors That Could Result in the Product |
|---|---|---|---|
| | | | |

**Round 3 Player B**

| Secret Multiplication Problem | Standard Form | Describe Product in Place Value Terms | Possible Factors That Could Result in the Product |
|---|---|---|---|
| | | | |

# LESSON 1.2 PRACTICE
## Using Place Value

**Directions:** Complete the problems below.

1. The following problem is missing two factors. You know one factor is a two-digit multiple of 10, and the other is a one-digit number.
   a. What are the missing factors? _____ × _____ = 560

   b. Are those the only possible factors? Explain.

2. While playing Mind Readers, two students disagreed on the multiplication problems that had a product of 36 tens. Player A said that 60 × 6 equals 36 tens, but Player B said that 4 × 90 equals 36 tens.
   a. Who do you agree with and why?

   b. Come up with another way to write 36 tens as a product.

3. While playing Mind Readers, two players disagreed on the multiplication problem. Student 1 said that the problem should have read 40 × 5 = 200, and Student 2 said that the problem should have read 50 × 4 = 200.
   a. Which student is correct? _____

   b. How do you know?

**4.** $5 \times 3 =$ _____ ones. Therefore, 50, or 5 _____ times 3 = 150 ones or 15 _____.

**5.** Explain the difference between 30 × 7 and 300 × 7.

## Extend Your Thinking

**1.** Multiply by multiples of 100 to determine products using place value knowledge.

**2.** Demonstrate each explanation using Base Ten blocks.

# LESSON 1.2
## Assessment Practice

1.  Explain how knowing the product of 3 × 8 will help you solve for the product of 3 × 80 and 8 × 30.

2.  The product of 60 × 2 is 12 tens. Write 12 tens in standard form.

3.  Knowing the product of 60 × 2 should help you determine the product of 6 × 2, which equals _____ ones, and 6 × 20, which equals _____ tens.

4.  Nehemiah says that 70 × 5 is 350 because 7 × 5 is 35, so you can just add a zero. Explain the reason behind adding the zero.

5.  What is the product of 40 × 5?

# LESSON 2.1 ACTIVITY
## Proper Placement of Properties

**Directions:** Pull one scenario card at a time out of the bag. With your group, discuss and solve the problem on the card. Then, categorize the card into one of the five properties of multiplication. Repeat these steps until all of the cards have been discussed, solved, and placed into a category.

### Extend Your Thinking

1. Could any of the scenario cards have been placed in more than one group? Explain your answer.

2. Determine if any properties of multiplication are also true for division. Think about the meaning of each property and apply it to a few division problems.

# Scenario Cards

1. Sammy made two 6 by 7 arrays and said (6 × 7) + (6 × 7) was equal to 2(6 × 7). Do you agree with Sammy? Explain why or why not.

   Explain to Sammy that to solve 2 × 6 × 7, he could have also made 7 different arrays, each representing the multiplication facts _____ × _____.

2. Carolina does not know the product of 12 × 11. She was told to decompose the 11 into 10 and 1, and then find the sum of 12 times 10 and 12 times 1. Write the expression that is described.

   Suggest another way to decompose 11 that would help Carolina multiply 12 times 11.

3. Knowing that 17 × 2 equals 34 can help Aaron solve 17 × 4 because he could decompose the 4 into _____ + _____.

   Write an equation that represents the equivalence of 17 × 4 and the decomposed expression.

4. Sue attempted to shoot the basketball into the net seven times on Monday, seven times on Tuesday, and seven times on Wednesday. She was unsuccessful with every attempt and described her experience as _____ shots with zero accuracy (21 × 0 = 0).

   Her coach said she should think of it as 0 successful attempts for _____ shots equals 0 points. Who is correct, Sue or her coach? Explain your answer.

**5.** When given six arrays, George took notes to help him discover a pattern, but he couldn't determine the rule for the pattern. Use the notes to explain to George the rule that supports this pattern.

| Array | Number of Rows | Number in Each Row | Product |
|-------|----------------|--------------------|---------|
| A | 7 | 1 | 7 |
| B | 27 | 1 | 27 |
| C | 1 | 54 | 54 |
| D | 1 | 12 | 12 |
| E | 19 | 1 | 19 |
| F | 81 | 1 | 81 |

**6.** Chastity is trying to determine the value of the variable N in the problem (8 × 6) + (N × 4) = 80. She knows that 8 × 6 = 48. Chastity also knows that 80 − 48 = 32. How can this help her determine the variable N?

**7.** In our numeral system, we have a unique number. No matter what you multiply this number by, it will always equal itself. What number is being described?

Can you think of any other unique numbers in our numeral system?

**8.** Draw two arrays to prove that the order in which the factors are multiplied does not affect the product. Use the product of 60.
- How many groups are in your first array?
- What is the size of each group in your first array?
- How many groups are in your second array?
- What is the size of each group in your second array?

**9.** Will zero groups of five have the same product as seven groups of zero? Explain your answer using number sentences or word sentences.

**10.** Rafael informed his teacher that he knew the product of 5 × 10 as well as the product of 5 × 6, but he didn't know the product of 16 × 5. The teacher told him to apply the facts he knew to solve the unknown multiplication product. How can Rafael use the two multiplication problems to determine the product of 16 × 5? Solve the problem.

**11.** Tamika knows all of the 3 multiplication facts from zero to 12, so therefore she knows that 3 × 6 = 18. When asked to solve 6 × 3, Tamika said she wasn't sure of the answer because she hasn't learned her 6 multiplication facts. Explain to Tamika that she does know what 6 × 3 is based on her knowledge of 3 × 6 equaling 18.

**12.** You are at a math contest, and you can only use numbers and signs, including =, ( ), +, −, ÷, and ×, to prove your thoughts. Following the contest rules, show that the way in which factors are grouped when being multiplied won't affect the product. Show this with the numbers 7, 8, and 9.

**13.** $14 \times 4 = 56$ and $14 \times 7 = 98$. Therefore, $14(4 + 7) =$ _____ + _____ = _____.

**14.** Laverne is trying to utilize a property of multiplication to help her solve $212 \times 15$. Laverne was informed that she could solve the problem in two different ways. Help her by filling in the blanks. $(212 \times 15) = (212 \times$ ___$) + (212 \times$ ___$)$ or $($___ $\times 15) + ($___ $\times 15)$.

Are these the only two ways that Laverne could use to help her solve $212 \times 15$? If not, how else could she have reached the product?

# LESSON 2.1 PRACTICE
## Multiplication

**Directions:** Complete the problems below.

1. Find the products below. What appears to be true about the order in which you multiply numbers? Prove your generalization by writing a problem to test your answer.

   a. $19 \times 8 =$ _____

      $8 \times 19 =$ _____

   b. $23 \times 7 =$ _____

      $7 \times 23 =$ _____

2. How could the fact that $7 \times 8 = 56$ and $2 \times 8 = 16$ help you calculate the product of $9 \times 8$?

3. Create the following word problems.
   a. Create a word problem that represents seven groups with 12 objects in each group.

   b. Create a word problem that represents 12 groups with seven objects in each.

**c.** What do you notice about Questions 3A and 3B? How is this related to the work you did in Question 1? How do you know?

4. $(7 \times 5) \times 2$ equals $7 \times (5 \times 2)$ but $(20 - 10) - 5$ does not equal $20 - (10 - 5)$. What can you conclude about the associative property based on this knowledge?

5. The school bought 6 boxes of red markers and 4 boxes of blue markers. If each box has 9 markers, how many markers did the school order in all? Show the product in two different ways using numbers, pictures, or words.

**Extend Your Thinking**

1. Create an example of a multiplication problem that is related to at least two properties of multiplication.

# LESSON 2.1

## Assessment Practice

**Directions:** Complete the problems below.

1. Which is the correct expression that describes the following array? Explain your reasoning.

   ```
   x x x x x
   x x x x x
   x x x x x
   ```

   a. $15 \times 3$
   b. $3 \times 5$
   c. $15 \times 5$
   d. $3 + 3$

2. Circle all that describe the following expression: $9 \times 8$.
   a. William had nine problems that each had eight steps to solve.
   b. William added nine 8 times.
   c. William had nine groups with eight in each.
   d. William had an array with nine rows of eight apples.

3. Mary Beth earns $8 every week that she weeds and waters the flower beds in her neighborhood. She does the work for 7 weeks. How much money does Mary Beth make weeding and watering the flowerbeds?
   a. $48
   b. $64
   c. $49
   d. $56

**4.** Which property of multiplication is being modeled in the following expression: $6 \times (4 + 3) = 6 \times 4 + 6 \times 3$

    **a.** Associative property of multiplication

    **b.** Distributive property of multiplication

    **c.** Identity property of multiplication

    **d.** Multiplicative property of one

**5.** Which of the following is not equivalent to $6 \times 13 \times 5$? What is wrong with the incorrect expression?

    **a.** $(6 \times 13)5$

    **b.** $(5 \times 13)6$

    **c.** $5 \times 18$

    **d.** $13(5 \times 6)$

# LESSON 2.2 ACTIVITY
## Multiply to Divide

**Directions:** With a partner, pull out all of the numbers and place them face up. Choose three numbers that will create a multiplication and division fact family. Lay the three numbers on the activity sheet, but do not glue the numbers yet.

Keep choosing three numbers at a time to create a fact family and place them on the activity sheet. If you get to the last three numbers, and they don't create a fact family, discuss how you can make changes so all of the numbers make fact families. All numbers must be used. Once you agree on the placement of all of the numbers, glue the numbers to the paper.

### Extend Your Thinking

1. Think of a number that could create at least two different fact families.

# LESSON 2.2
## Fact Families

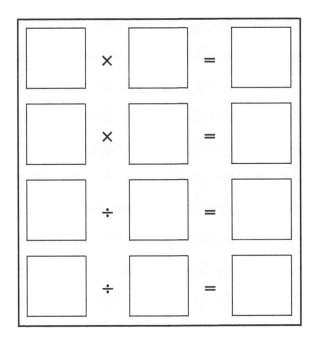

# Number Cards

| | | | | | |
|---|---|---|---|---|---|
| 8 | 10 | 4 | 7 | 32 | 70 |
| 16 | 2 | 4 | 9 | 4 | 18 |
| 36 | 36 | 6 | 6 | 6 | 6 |
| 15 | 70 | 3 | 10 | 5 | 7 |
| 18 | 18 | 9 | 2 | 2 | 9 |
| 7 | 16 | 10 | 4 | 70 | 4 |
| 32 | 15 | 4 | 5 | 8 | 3 |
| 6 | 70 | 6 | 7 | 36 | 10 |
| 5 | 32 | 3 | 8 | 15 | 4 |
| 36 | 18 | 6 | 9 | 6 | 2 |
| 4 | 32 | 4 | 8 | 16 | 4 |
| 16 | 3 | 4 | 5 | 4 | 15 |

# LESSON 2.2 PRACTICE
## Division

**Directions:** Complete the problems below.

1.  Because you know 16 × 7, or 16 groups of 7, equals 112, you also know that 112 has how many groups of 16? Show your answer using a number bond.

2.  There are many different fact families that can be used to represent the number 32. The number 16 can be multiplied by _____, and the number 8 can be multiplied by _____. Therefore, you know that 32 can be divided evenly by what numbers? Write the fact families you used to arrive at your answer.

3.  Draw an array and write a multiplication equation to represent 54 divided into nine groups. How many are in each group? _____

**4.** Two hundred and twenty-five Skittles are divided into equal groups.

    **a.** Suppose you divide the number of Skittles equally among 25 students in your class. How many Skittles does each person get? _____

    **b.** Divide 225 into a different number of groups than in Part A. How many groups did you divide 225 into? _____ What was the size of the groups? _____ What is a multiplication equation you could use to represent your problem? _____ Write a related division equation. _____

    **c.** What is another way to divide the Skittles evenly?

    **d.** Suppose your teacher would like to have some Skittles also, meaning you need to divide the 225 Skittles into 26 groups. How should you do this?

**5.** How many times can you subtract 11 from 110? Write the related division equation.

**6.** Solve for the missing factor, and then write the related division equation.

    **a.** $4 \times$ _____ $= 28$

    **b.** _____ $\times 12 = 36$

    **c.** $18 =$ _____ $\times 6$

    **d.** What can you infer about the numbers 36 and 18 from Parts B and C based on the missing factor of each problem? Give another example of a number that fits this pattern.

# LESSON 2.2
## Assessment Practice

**Directions:** Complete the problems below.

1. Raphael has 24 flowers to distribute evenly among 4 flower arrangements. How many flowers will be in each arrangement? _____ Which expression represents the above problem? How do you know?

   a. $24 \times 4 =$ _____

   b. $4 \times 24 =$ _____

   c. $24 \div 4 =$ _____

   d. $4 \div 24 =$ _____

2. A grocery store has 21 canned goods that need to be placed evenly on the shelves. There are a total of 3 shelves. How many canned goods should be placed on each shelf? _____ Circle all of the expressions that can be used to solve the above problem. Explain your reasoning.

   a. $3 \div 21 =$ _____

   b. $3 \times n = 21$

   c. $21 \div 3 =$ _____

   d. $3 \div n = 21$

3. Which expression could be used to help you solve $64 \div 8$? How could this expression help you?
   a. $8 \times N$
   b. $64 \times 8$
   c. $8 \times 64$
   d. $8 \div 64$

4. Solve for the unknown: $30 \div 6 = N$. Circle your answer below. Draw a picture to show how you arrived at your answer.
   a. $N = 180$
   b. $N = 6$
   c. $N = 36$
   d. $N = 5$

5. Which equation could help you solve for the unknown factor in $8 \times P = 32$? How would you use the equation?
   a. $32 \times 8 = P$
   b. $8 \times 32 = P$
   c. $P = 32 \div 8$
   d. $P = 8 \div 32$

6. Peter says that 108 can be divided into 9 equal groups. Kayla says that 108 can be divided into 2 equal groups. Which student is correct? How do you know?

# LESSON 2.3 ACTIVITY
# Make the Match

**Directions:** It's time to test your memory skills as well as your knowledge of properties. Be ready to take a picture with your mind of various expressions. With a partner, pull all of the expressions out of the bag and place them face down in front of you. Play memory by choosing two expressions that are equivalent and can be joined to create an equation. Matches will be based on properties and strategies you have learned.

Continue matching the expressions based on properties and strategies until all of the equations have been created. Prove the expressions are equivalent by solving each side of the problems. Glue each equation to the corresponding recording sheet based on the represented property or strategy. Be sure to check the work of your partner as they are working.

## Extend Your Thinking

1. Look at the division expressions. The original division problem has been broken into two smaller division problems. With your partner, decide if the problem could have been broken up into any other combinations and record those on your sheet.

2. Use the equations on the Distributive Property recording sheet to help you solve the following question: How could the fact that 10 – 1 = 9 help you solve 9 × 25?

## Equations/Answer Sheet

| | |
|---|---|
| $(11 \times 2) + (11 \times 10)$ | $11 \times 12$ |
| $64 \div 8$ | $8 \times n = 64$ |
| $25 \times 7$ | $(20 + 5) \times 7$ |
| $45 \times 4$ | $4 \times 45$ |
| $48 \div 6$ | $(30 \div 6) + (18 \div 6)$ |
| $9 \times 6 \times 7$ | $(9 \times 6)7$<br>or<br>$(6 \times 7)9$<br>or<br>$(7 \times 9)6$ |
| $6(7 + 8)$ | $(6 \times 7) + (6 \times 8)$ |
| $4 \times 3 \times 6$ | $(4 \times 3)6$<br>or<br>$(3 \times 6) \times 4$<br>or<br>$(4 \times 6) \times 3$ |
| $32 \div n = 8$ | $8 \times n = 32$ |
| $n \times 6 = 36$ | $36 \div 6 = n$ |
| $54 \div 6 = n$ | $6 \times n = 54$ |
| $73 \times 4$ | Multiply $73 \times 2$, and then double the product |
| $79 \times 10$ | $790 \div 2 = 79 \times 5$ |
| $37 \times 9$ | $(37 \times 10) - (37 \times 1)$ |

# LESSON 2.3 RECORDING SHEET
## Distributive Property

|  | = |  |
|---|---|---|
|  | = |  |
|  | = |  |
|  | = |  |
|  | = |  |
|  | = |  |

# LESSON 2.3 RECORDING SHEET
## Commutative Property

|  | = |  |
|---|---|---|
|  | = |  |
|  | = |  |
|  | = |  |
|  | = |  |
|  | = |  |

# LESSON 2.3 RECORDING SHEET

## Associative Property

| | | |
|---|---|---|
| | = | |
| | = | |
| | = | |
| | = | |
| | = | |
| | = | |

## Inverse Operations

|  | = |  |
|---|:---:|---|
|  | = |  |
|  | = |  |
|  | = |  |
|  | = |  |
|  | = |  |

# LESSON 2.3 RECORDING SHEET
## Strategies and Additional Problems

| | | |
|---|---|---|
| | = | |
| | = | |
| | = | |
| | = | |
| | = | |
| | = | |

# LESSON 2.3 PRACTICE
# Multiplication and Division

1. Suppose your classmate does not know the product of 16 groups of 4. How might you help your friend calculate this answer by regrouping?

2. Read and study the following table. Then use the product of a number times 2 and the product of a number times 4 to help you create a rule for mentally solving a number times 8. Once you have discovered the rule, fill in the missing values (x, p, e, and n) in the table. What appears to be the relationship between a number times 4 and that same number times 8?

| Number | Multiplied by 2 | Multiplied by 4 | Multiplied by 8 |
|--------|-----------------|-----------------|-----------------|
| 5 | 10 | 20 | x |
| 9 | 18 | p | 72 |
| 7 | 14 | 28 | e |
| 3 | n | 12 | 24 |

3. How does the rule you just described in the table above help you solve $67 \times 8$?

4. Apply the rule you just created to the following problems to check their accuracy.

   a. $4 \times 4 = (4 \times 2)n$

   n = _____

   b. $4 \times 6 = (2 \times 6)n$

   n = _____

5. How could Sedrick use the fact that $40 \times 8 = 320$ to help him determine the product of $47 \times 8$?

# LESSON 2.3

## Assessment Practice

**Directions:** Complete the problems below.

1. $56 = 8 \times N$
   a. $N = 9$
   b. $N = 7$
   c. $N = 8$
   d. $N = 6$

2. Maria has 3 boxes of candles. There are a total of 36 candles.
   a. If all of the candles are split equally among the boxes, how many candles are in each box? _____

   b. Which two expressions could be used to solve the previous problem?
      i. $3 = 36 \times C$
      ii. $36 = 3 \div C$
      iii. $36 = C \times 3$
      iv. $36 \div 3 = C$

   c. Explain your answer. How can both expressions be used to solve the problem?

3. 6 groups of n equals 42. n = _____
   a. 7
   b. 9
   c. 4
   d. 8

4. Skip count by 4 seven times. Demonstrate your skip counting on the number line provided. Skip counting by 4 seven times will result in what number? _____

5. Select which division expression can be used to solve the following problem: $3 \times 12 = 36$.
   a. $12 \div 3$
   b. $36 \div 12$
   c. $3 \div 12$
   d. $12 \div 36$

# LESSON 2.4 ACTIVITY
# Architect Arithmetic

**Directions:** Suppose you are no longer a student in this classroom, but instead an architect who is constructing a replica of a famous building. With a partner, choose one of the four famous buildings that you would like to construct, or one based on your own interests, and answer the questions on the corresponding building sheet. Use the information on the building sheet to help you build.

## BUILDING OPTIONS

| **The Leaning Tower of Pisa**<br>**Location:** Pisa, Italy<br>**Height:** 56 meters | **The Eiffel Tower**<br>**Location:** Paris, France<br>**Height:** Approximately 300 meters |
|---|---|
| **The Statue of Liberty**<br>**Location:** New York, New York<br>**Height:** Approximately 90 meters | **The Great Pyramid**<br>**Location:** El Giza, Egypt<br>**Height:** 450 feet |
| _____<br><br>Location: _____<br><br>Height: _____ | _____<br><br>Location: _____<br><br>Height: _____ |

You will be given a set of toothpicks to use. Each toothpick stands for a certain length, so be sure to use the information carefully. Construct your building by gluing the toothpicks to your construction paper. The building will be a scaled model, which means it won't be the real height, but it will be an accurate model. The width of the building is your choice.

## Extend Your Thinking

1. For each of the four buildings, determine a different amount that each toothpick could represent. There should be no remainders, and no toothpicks should be cut.

# LESSON 2.4 ACTIVITY & PRACTICE
# Building Sheet

## THE LEANING TOWER OF PISA
Location: Pisa, Italy
Height: 56 meters tall

You are the architect in charge of building a replica of the Leaning Tower of Pisa. Use the information and questions below to help plan your building.

1. The toothpicks each stand for 7 meters.
   a. How many toothpicks will you need to construct one side of the building that would represent the height of 56 meters? _____ Write an equation using a variable to represent the unknown. Solve.

   b. Prove your answer is reasonable.

Use the toothpicks that represent 7 meters each to build the Leaning Tower of Pisa. Remember to make sure the height represents 56 meters. After building the replica, answer the following questions.

2. If you were building the actual Leaning Tower of Pisa rather than a scaled model, it would have taken you a lot longer. Research how long it took to build the actual Leaning Tower of Pisa. If you were to break up the building process into 3 different time frames, how long would each time frame be?

3. You have been hired to paint a wall in the Leaning Tower of Pisa. The wall stands 56 meters tall and is 3 meters wide. To determine the amount of area on the plane figure that you must paint, you must multiply 56 meters by 3 meters. What is the product? _____

**4.** You decide to paint it in 28 days. How many square meters of the wall would you need to paint each day? _____

**5.** You only get paid every 14 square meters of painting. How many paychecks will you receive after completing the entire painting job? _____

**6.** If each paycheck equals $2,751.29, what is the grand total you will make for your replica? _____

**7.** If you needed $40,000.00 to start the next project, how much more money do you need to earn? _____

# LESSON 2.4 ACTIVITY & PRACTICE
## Building Sheet

### THE EIFFEL TOWER
Location: Paris, France
Height: Approximately 300 meters tall

You are the architect in charge of building a replica of the Eiffel Tower. Use the information and questions below to help plan your building.

1. The toothpicks each stand for 20 meters.
   a. How many toothpicks will you need to construct one side of the building that would represent the height of 300 meters? _____ Write an equation using a variable to represent the unknown. Solve.

   b. Prove your answer is reasonable.

Use the toothpicks that represent 20 meters each to build the Eiffel Tower. Remember to make sure the height represents 300 meters. After building the replica, answer the following questions.

2. For every 10 meters completed, you receive an extra day of vacation time.
   a. How many extra days of vacation time can you earn on this project? _____ Write an equation using a variable to represent the unknown. Solve.

   b. Use the inverse operation to check your work.

3. The Eiffel Tower has 1,665 steps from the East Pillar to the top. You have been asked to replace all of them. Because this is such a tiring job, you are trying to schedule yourself breaks every so often.

   a. If you wanted to take a break after an equal number of steps, what options do you have? List as many as you can think of. (Hint: Think about divisibility rules. For example, I know I could rest after each set of 5 steps because 5 goes evenly into 1,665.)

   b. Choose one of your answers from Part A. How many breaks would you take? _____

4. You have been asked to consider building more steps. If you needed a total of 2,000 steps, how many more steps would you have to build? _____ Use addition to prove your answer is reasonable.

# LESSON 2.4 ACTIVITY & PRACTICE
# Building Sheet

## THE STATUE OF LIBERTY
Location: New York, New York
Height: Approximately 90 meters tall

You are the architect in charge of building a replica of the Statue of Liberty. Use the information and questions below to help plan your building.

1. The toothpicks each stand for 5 meters.
   a. How many toothpicks will you need to construct one side of the building that would represent the height of 90 meters? _____ Write an equation using a variable to represent the unknown. Solve.

   b. Prove your answer is reasonable.

Use the toothpicks that represent 5 meters each to build the Statue of Liberty. Remember to make sure the height represents 90 meters. After building the replica, answer the following questions.

2. You have decided to build the replica in two different sections. Each part is equivalent in height.
   a. What is the height of each section? _____ Write an equation using a variable to represent the unknown. Solve.

   b. Use the inverse operation to check your work.

3. You decide to cover the front face of the tablet with copper. The front of the tablet is about 24 feet tall and about 14 feet wide. To decide how many square feet of copper you need to fill the plane surface, you must multiply 24 feet by 14 feet.
   a. What is the product? _____

   b. Write a division equation to check your work.

4. You were given two paychecks worth $1,274 each for building the Statue of Liberty replica. You were also given one paycheck worth $984.99 for painting the Statue of Liberty replica.
   a. How much total money did you make for building and painting the Statue of Liberty?

   b. How much more money did you get paid for building the statue than for painting the statue?

# LESSON 2.4 ACTIVITY & PRACTICE
## Building Sheet

### THE GREAT PYRAMID
Location: El Giza, Egypt
Height: 450 feet tall

You are the architect in charge of building a replica of the Great Pyramid. Use the information and questions below to help plan your building.

1. The toothpicks each stand for 45 feet.
   a. How many toothpicks will you need to construct one side of the building that would represent the height of 450 feet? _____ Write an equation using a variable to represent the unknown. Solve.

   b. Prove your answer is reasonable.

Use the toothpicks that represent 45 feet each to build the Great Pyramid. Remember to make sure the height represents 450 feet. After building the replica, answer the following questions.

2. You have decided to build the replica in five different but equal sections. Each part is equivalent in height.
   a. What is the height of each section? _____ Write an equation using a variable to represent the unknown. Solve.

   b. Use the inverse operation to check your work.

3. The base of the pyramid is 755 feet long.
   a. How much wider is the base of the pyramid than the height of the pyramid?
   _____

   b. Prove your answer is reasonable.

4. Leading into the Great Pyramid, there is an entranceway that leads to an underground chamber that is about 190 feet deep.
   a. If you were in charge of building doorways every 5 feet, and were paid $75 for each door, how much money would you make? _____

   b. If you had 3 employees helping you build the doorways, and each employee was paid $150.00, how much money would you have left? _____

# LESSON 2.4

## Assessment Practice

**Directions:** Complete the problems below.

1. Rebekah has 42 gloves in her closet. How many pair of gloves does she have?
   a. 22
   b. 12
   c. 21
   d. 84

2. Janiya brought donuts to give to her teachers for breakfast one morning. She brought 2-dozen donuts. Janiya gave each teacher 6 donuts. How many teachers did Janiya give donuts to?
   a. 6
   b. 5
   c. 4
   d. 12

3. Jonas has 84 baseball cards. He splits the cards evenly between 14 friends. How many cards does each friend receive?
   a. 7
   b. 6
   c. 3
   d. 5

4. The library has placed 74 books equally on 2 shelves. How many books are on each shelf? Write the multiplication equation using the variable $b$ to represent the unknown.

5. When trying to determine the answer to Question 4, a student raised her hand and said that multiplication isn't the mathematical operation that should be used, so the problem can't be solved. Instead, she thought division should be used. How would you respond to this student if you were the teacher?

    *Math Curriculum for Gifted Students, Grade 3, Sections I–II*

# LESSON 2.5 ACTIVITY
## Chef's Choice

**Directions:** Your expertise in math is needed to help people! You have now become a well-known chef in a large city at a popular restaurant. With a partner, you will create a menu for people based on their dietary needs. Choose one Meal Request Card at a time and read the request. Use the Food Fact Sheet to create a meal based on the needs and requests located on the card. Once you have discussed and chosen items, fill in the menu. Repeat these steps until all meal request cards have been completed.

### Extend Your Thinking

The following are ideas for extending the activity:

1. Look at each menu you created and the corresponding meal request card. Are the options you chose the only options? If not, list the options for each category that each person could have received and still followed their calorie limit.

2. Research the daily caloric intake of boys and girls ages 9–14 and then create a corresponding meal based on the data obtained.

# LESSON 2.5
# Meal Request Cards

| | |
|---|---|
| **1.** I am only allowed 1,090 calories per meal. I cannot go over that amount and will be hungry if I eat less than 1,085 calories a meal.<br><br>My request is:<br>1 meat<br>1 vegetable<br>1 sweet<br><br><br><br>If I am cooking for two others and myself, what is the total amount of calories for each category?<br>Meat:<br>Vegetable:<br>Sweet: | **2.** I am only allowed 1,560 calories for my supper. I cannot go over that number and will be hungry if I eat much less than 1,560 calories at supper.<br><br>My request is at least:<br>2 meats<br>1 fruit<br>1 vegetable<br>2 carbohydrates<br>1 sweet<br><br>If I am cooking for four others and myself, what is the total amount of calories for each category?<br>Meat:<br>Fruit:<br>Vegetable:<br>Carbohydrates:<br>Sweet: |
| **3.** I am only allowed between 770–780 calories for lunch.<br><br>My request is:<br>2 servings of chicken<br>1 fruit<br>1 vegetable<br><br>If I am cooking one serving of chicken for each of the 7 members of my family plus the 2 servings that I will eat, how many total calories of chicken are being cooked? | **4.** I decide to eat 609 calories at lunch. My main meal must be spaghetti.<br><br>My request is:<br>1 serving of spaghetti<br>1 carbohydrate<br>1 sweet<br><br>If I decide to add a vegetable to my lunch but want to eat no more than 641 calories, what will I eat? |

# LESSON 2.5
# Food Fact Sheet

The provided calorie amounts are based on one serving and were obtained from http://caloriecount.com.

### Meats

**Steak:** 847 cal.
**Chicken:** 306 cal.
**Spaghetti:** 221 cal.
**Ham:** 736 cal.
**Turkey:** 45 cal.

### Fruits

**Cantaloupe:** 60 cal.
**Strawberries:** 47 cal.
**Apple:** 95 cal.

### Vegetables

**Broccoli:** 50 cal.
**Sweet potato:** 114 cal.
**Zucchini:** 33 cal.
**Tomato:** 32 cal.
**Cauliflower:** 146 cal.

### Carbohydrates

**Roll:** 87 cal.
**Rice:** 216 cal.
**Baked potato:** 129 cal.

### Sweets

**Chocolate pie:** 301 cal.
**Pecan pie:** 117 cal.

# LESSON 2.5
## Menu

**Meats:**

**Fruits:**

**Vegetables:**

**Carbohydrates:**

**Sweets:**

# LESSON 2.5 PRACTICE
## Multistep Word Problems

**Directions:** Complete the problems below.

1. A small package of Sun Chips has 140 calories. The bag Timothy enjoyed contained 20 chips.
   a. If Timothy gave Kevin 4 chips, how many calories did Kevin consume? _____

   b. How many calories did Timothy consume? _____

   c. How many more calories did Timothy consume than Kevin? _____

2. The small bag of Cheetos contains 150 calories. There are 25 chips in the bag.
   a. How many calories does each chip have? _____

   b. How many chips should you give away if you are on a diet that requires only a 75-calorie snack? _____ Use the variable c to represent the unknown number of chips given away. Explain how you know your answer is reasonable.

3. One bag of Fritos has 160 calories. There are 20 chips in a bag.
   a. If you wanted to share the calories evenly among some friends, how many friends could receive an equal amount of calories? _____ Think of as many options as you can and prove your answer is reasonable.

   b. If Dexter only wanted to consume 120 calories, how many chips should he discard? _____

**Extend Your Thinking**

1. Choose a snack item and look at the nutrition label. Create questions about the food product that will make your classmates add, subtract, multiply, or divide to solve.

2. Look up the dietary guidelines for caloric intakes per day for adults. Then design meals using caloriecount.com that reflect the caloric intake guidelines for adults. Finally, create a menu that displays your meal options.

# LESSON 2.5
# Assessment Practice

**Directions:** Complete the problems below.

1. For the swimming party, Julia's mom is filling old baby pools with water. Every time she fills 8 pools, she discovers leaks in half of the pools. How many pools does Julia's mom need to fill if she must have 72 baby pools full of water?

2. Fifty-four people came to the Dinosaur Science night. Each of the 54 students created 3 fossil molds. If 14 of the fossil molds broke, how many fossil molds were not broken?

3. Penelope made 75 brownies for teacher appreciation week at her school. She brought 16 on Monday, 23 on Tuesday, and the rest on Wednesday. How many brownies did Penelope bring to school on Wednesday?

4. During class economy day, Alicia purchased 4 basketballs for $14 each. She paid for the basketballs with three $20 bills. How much change did Alicia receive?

5. Susie, Beth, and Carlos decided to combine their money to buy a gift for their parents. Susie has $23, Beth has three times as much as Susie, and Carlos has $9 less than Beth. How much money does Carlos have?

# LESSON 2.6 ACTIVITY
## What's the Pattern?

**Directions:** Input/output charts are just like puzzles. Your powerful puzzle skills are needed to place numbers in the correct places depending on given clues. Work with a partner and choose a What's the Pattern? Chart and gather the bag of corresponding number cards.

Use the clues given to solve the puzzle by filling in the blanks with the numbers. Place all of the numbers so you and your partner can see them. Once you have made all of the input/output matches, place them in order from least to greatest. Glue the numbers to the chart, and then answer the questions.

### Extend Your Thinking

1.  You should have discovered patterns that occur when multiplying and adding by certain numbers. See if you can find any patterns dealing with division. What happens when you divide an even number by an even number? What about when you divide an even number by an odd number? An odd number by an even number?

2.  Create your own input/output chart with numbers in the correct place and have a partner determine the rule.

| Input | Output |
|---|---|
|  |  |
|  |  |
|  |  |
|  |  |

# LESSON 2.6
# What's the Pattern? Chart 1

The rule for the chart is to add 7.

| Input | Output |
|---|---|
|  |  |
|  |  |
|  |  |
|  |  |
|  |  |

1. Once you have filled in the chart, look for a pattern for adding even and odd numbers. What do you notice about the sum of an even number plus an odd number?

2. Generate a few more number sentences to check to see that your hypothesis is correct.

## What's the Pattern? Number Cards 1

| | |
|:---:|:---:|
| 2 | 9 |
| 4 | 11 |
| 6 | 13 |
| 8 | 15 |
| 10 | 17 |

# LESSON 2.6
## What's the Pattern? Chart 2

The rule for the chart is to multiply by 3.

| Input | Output |
|-------|--------|
|       |        |
|       |        |
|       |        |
|       |        |
|       |        |
|       |        |

1. Use the information in the chart to help you answer the following questions.
   a. What do you notice about multiplying an odd number times an even number?

   b. What do you notice about multiplying an odd number times an odd number?

2. Generate some number sentences of your own to check your hypothesis.

# What's the Pattern? Number Cards 2

| 7 | 21 |
|---|---|
| 10 | 30 |
| 13 | 39 |
| 16 | 48 |
| 19 | 57 |
| 22 | 66 |

# LESSON 2.6
## What's the Pattern? Chart 3

The rule for the chart is to multiply by 4.

| Input | Output |
|-------|--------|
|       |        |
|       |        |
|       |        |
|       |        |
|       |        |
|       |        |

1. Look for a pattern in the output side of the table.
   a. What do you notice?



   b. What do you notice about multiplying an odd number times an even number?



2. Bradley doesn't know what 34 × 4 equals. Tony told him to calculate 34 × 2 and then double the product. Do you agree with Tony? Why or why not? Provide an example to support your answer.

# What's the Pattern? Number Cards 3

| | |
|---|---|
| 1 | 4 |
| 2 | 8 |
| 3 | 12 |
| 4 | 16 |
| 5 | 20 |
| 6 | 24 |

# LESSON 2.6 PRACTICE
## Patterns

**Directions:** Complete the problems below.

1. On the completed multiplication chart provided, highlight one row and one column that show the order in which factors are multiplied doesn't change the product.

2. On the blank multiplication sheet provided, use the following colors to solve certain facts.
   a. Solve all of the even numbers times even numbers in blue. What do you notice about the products?

   b. Solve all of the even numbers times odd numbers in red. What do you notice about the products?

   c. Solve all of the odd numbers times odd numbers in green. What do you notice about the products?

3. Now think about addition. Do you think the patterns of odd and even number products will be the same for the sum of numbers? Support your answer with evidence.

**Extend Your Thinking**

1. Analyze the multiplication chart to discover more patterns created. Highlight your patterns in a different color.

# Completed Multiplication Chart

| X | 0 | 1 | 2 | 3 | 4 | 5 | 6 | 7 | 8 | 9 | 10 | 11 | 12 |
|---|---|---|---|---|---|---|---|---|---|---|----|----|----|
| 0 | 0 | 0 | 0 | 0 | 0 | 0 | 0 | 0 | 0 | 0 | 0 | 0 | 0 |
| 1 | 0 | 1 | 2 | 3 | 4 | 5 | 6 | 7 | 8 | 9 | 10 | 11 | 12 |
| 2 | 0 | 2 | 4 | 6 | 8 | 10 | 12 | 14 | 16 | 18 | 20 | 22 | 24 |
| 3 | 0 | 3 | 6 | 9 | 12 | 15 | 18 | 21 | 24 | 27 | 30 | 33 | 36 |
| 4 | 0 | 4 | 8 | 12 | 16 | 20 | 24 | 28 | 32 | 36 | 40 | 44 | 48 |
| 5 | 0 | 5 | 10 | 15 | 20 | 25 | 30 | 35 | 40 | 45 | 50 | 55 | 60 |
| 6 | 0 | 6 | 12 | 18 | 24 | 30 | 36 | 42 | 48 | 54 | 60 | 66 | 72 |
| 7 | 0 | 7 | 14 | 21 | 28 | 35 | 42 | 49 | 56 | 63 | 70 | 77 | 84 |
| 8 | 0 | 8 | 16 | 24 | 32 | 40 | 48 | 56 | 64 | 72 | 80 | 88 | 96 |
| 9 | 0 | 9 | 18 | 27 | 36 | 45 | 54 | 63 | 72 | 81 | 90 | 99 | 108 |
| 10 | 0 | 10 | 20 | 30 | 40 | 50 | 60 | 70 | 80 | 90 | 100 | 110 | 120 |
| 11 | 0 | 11 | 22 | 33 | 44 | 55 | 66 | 77 | 88 | 99 | 110 | 121 | 132 |
| 12 | 0 | 12 | 24 | 36 | 48 | 60 | 72 | 84 | 96 | 108 | 120 | 132 | 144 |

Section II: Operations and Algebraic Thinking

# LESSON 2.6

## Blank Multiplication Chart

| X | 0 | 1 | 2 | 3 | 4 | 5 | 6 | 7 | 8 | 9 | 10 | 11 | 12 |
|----|---|---|---|---|---|---|---|---|---|---|----|----|----|
| 0 | | | | | | | | | | | | | |
| 1 | | | | | | | | | | | | | |
| 2 | | | | | | | | | | | | | |
| 3 | | | | | | | | | | | | | |
| 4 | | | | | | | | | | | | | |
| 5 | | | | | | | | | | | | | |
| 6 | | | | | | | | | | | | | |
| 7 | | | | | | | | | | | | | |
| 8 | | | | | | | | | | | | | |
| 9 | | | | | | | | | | | | | |
| 10 | | | | | | | | | | | | | |
| 11 | | | | | | | | | | | | | |
| 12 | | | | | | | | | | | | | |

# LESSON 2.6

## Assessment Practice

**Directions:** Complete the problems below.

1. Write a four-number pattern, starting at any number you choose, that follows this rule: Multiply by 7.

2. What is the rule to the following pattern?

    1,654;        1,634;        1,614;        1,594

   a. Multiply by 2
   b. Divide by 2
   c. Add 12
   d. Subtract 20

3. The following pattern was created by multiplying each number by n. What does n equal?

    15,        45,        135,        405

   a. n = 3
   b. n = 5
   c. n = 7
   d. n = 2

4. Selma mowed lawns for extra money. The table shows the amount of yards mowed and the amount of money earned. If Selma continues to be paid in the same way, fill in the rest of the chart.

| Lawns Mowed | Money |
| --- | --- |
| 1 | $19.00 |
| 2 | $26.00 |
| 3 | |
| 4 | |
| 5 | $47.00 |
| 6 | |